Totally AMAZING RAIN FORESTS

 A GOLDEN BOOK • NEW YORK

Golden Books Publishing Company, Inc., New York, New York 10106

Created by Two-Can for Golden Books Publishing Company, Inc. Copyright © 1998 Golden Books Publishing Company, Inc. All rights reserved.
Printed in the USA. No part of this book may be reproduced or copied in any form without written permission from the copyright owner.
GOLDEN BOOKS®, A GOLDEN BOOK®, TOTALLY AMAZING™, and G DESIGN™ are trademarks of
Golden Books Publishing Company, Inc. Library of Congress Catalog Card Number: 98–84144
ISBN: 0-307-20163-5   A MCMXCVIII

Journey into the Jungle

Are you ready to join an expedition into the amazing world of the steaming-hot rain forest, where it rains nearly every single day? Trees tower high in the sky and amazing animals live everywhere—from the trees' tops to their tangled roots.

That's Weird

There are so many different kinds of rain forest animals that scientists have not given them all names yet.

What's your name?

Where in the World?

Rain forests don't grow just anywhere. They are found in the hottest places in the world, which lie near the equator, an imaginary line that goes all the way around the middle of Earth.

Leafy Layers

A rain forest is divided into three layers. The leafy layer at the top of the trees is called the canopy. Below the canopy, smaller plants grow in the understory. The forest floor is damp, dark, and a bit spooky!

Giant trees peep out above the canopy.

Monkeys swing and birds fly in the canopy.

Frogs hop and snakes slither in the understory.

Jaguars prowl and insects march on the forest floor.

△ Each kind of animal has a favorite spot to make its home in the layers of the rain forest.

▲ The Amazon River snakes through the huge Amazon Rain Forest, which is almost as big as Australia.

Life at the Top

Birds that live in the canopy spend their time flying and squawking among the branches, stocking up on ripe fruit and nuts. Their feet never need to touch the ground.

Beak Cool!

The toucan's colorful beak, or bill, has many uses. It's great for reaching those hard-to-get berries, slicing through chunks of fresh fruit, and even for playing games of catch with other toucans. Its beak is so bright, it also makes a fantastic flag that helps attract a mate and warns other birds not to steal its eggs.

Success Story

When a bird eats fruit, some seeds end up in its droppings. Eventually, the seeds grow into new plants.

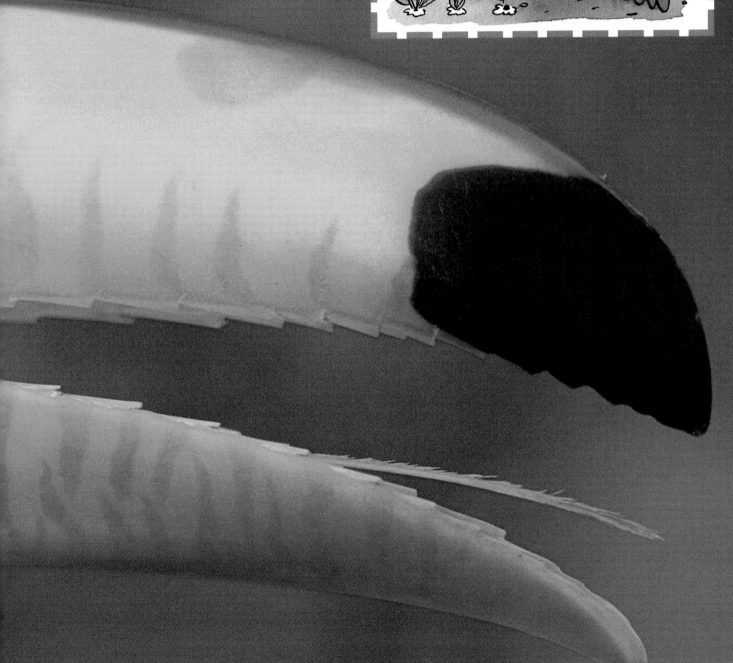

▲ A toucan's beak isn't as heavy as it looks. It's mainly a hollow shell.

Flower Power!

From a lily big enough for a family picnic to a towering orchid—rain forest plants are extraordinary. Insects are attracted to plants by their color and their odor, which can be sweet or really sour.

High Flyer

Rain forest orchids have inside-out roots. Instead of being underground the roots trail in the air and soak up moisture. The plants grow high up on the tallest trees. The flowers are a real hit with animals, especially insects, who drink the sweet nectar.

▲ This tree frog has found its own orchid swimming pool.

GREEN & GORGEOUS

Record Breaker

The prize for the biggest flower goes to the giant rafflesia that grows on the forest floor in parts of Asia. It can be as wide as you are tall, but it's no beauty. It has thick warty petals and a spiky center that stinks of rotting meat. The smell attracts swarms of flies.

That's Weird

Male bees flock to the bucket orchid to gather a goo that is sure to impress female bees. The male rubs it on his legs, then flies off in search of a hot date!

Yumm!

Feeling Fruity

The durian is the smelliest fruit in the rain forest. Its stench of rotten fish drifts up to half a mile away. When the durian is ripe, animals smell it out, then feast on the stinky fruit. Many people think that the durian tastes delicious, too.

The chewing gum you blow into bubbles is made from chicle, which comes from sapodilla trees in the Amazon Rain Forest.

Rubber starts off as a milky juice which flows from a rubber tree. But it ends up as bouncy, stretchy stuff, perfect for making all kinds of things, from footballs and bicycle tires to wet suits.

Animal Chatters

Rain forest animals have plenty to talk about. Frogs croak, monkeys whoop, and birds screech, which is their way of saying "Hi!" to friends and "Go away" to enemies.

Phew! I'm running out of air!

Strange but True
The Cuban arrow frog is only half an inch (1.2 cm) long. That's about the size of a small grape.

Frog Chorus

All kinds of male frogs serenade female frogs with deep throaty croaks. The male with the loudest booming croak wins the affection of the female. Frogs also croak to tell enemies to hop off!

Crrroak!

▲ This frog can stretch the skin under its chin like a balloon to make its croak mega-loud!

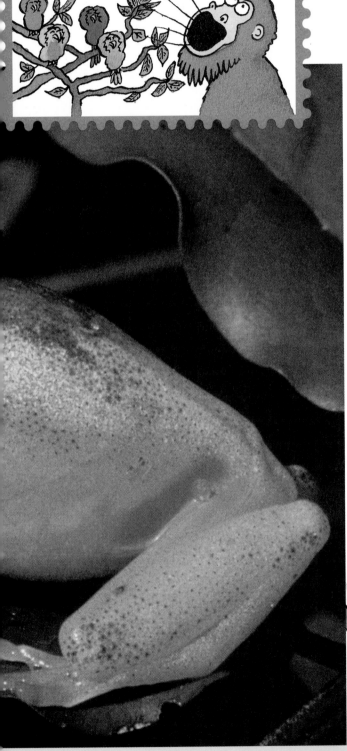

A Nose for Noise

The male proboscis monkey has a long droopy growth for its nose, which he "plays" loudly like a trumpet. He lets other monkeys in his group know that he's boss by warning them of danger and calling them together for meetings.

Tuneful Gibbons

Gibbons are musical animals. When male and female gibbons mate, they stay friends forever and sing duets to one another. A family of gibbons also calls across the canopy to keep other families away from its patch.

Rain forest animals have some strange ideas about setting up a home and starting a family. Most leave their young to look after themselves, but others take great care of them.

Forest Families

BACHELOR BIRDHOUSE

The male bower bird makes a fancy house with matching flowers and feathers to attract a female bird.

This spot is just perfect.

Then he adds a splash of color with berry juice.

SQUASHED BERRIES

I like this shade of blue.

When the house is ready, he waits inside for a female bower bird.

Well, hello!

I like your house.

Strange but True

Chimpanzees live in close-knit families. They groom each other's fur, hold hands, and even kiss each other!

Gorilla Picnic

Each morning, the father gorilla, called the silverback, wakes up the family to enjoy a meal of fruit, leaves, and bark. After breakfast, the grown-ups snooze while the young play games. The young gorillas will stay with their parents until they are more than ten years old.

▼ A mother sloth hangs upside down from a tree by her toes. Her baby holds on tight.

I'm just hanging around.

Lazy Baby

There's no pressure on a baby sloth to leave home. Each long-haired sloth baby spends six to nine months hanging on to the fur on its mother's stomach. Then the lazy-bones moves off on its own, extremely slowly, to find its own tree, where it may live for years and years.

Hey, Dad Just Swallowed the Kids!

Being a dad is a serious business for the male Darwin frog. When the eggs hatch into tadpoles, he scoops them up and carries them around in a pouch in his mouth. After about three weeks, the proud dad spits out the little froglets, who can now hop around by themselves!

11

Fruits of the Forest

What's on the menu in the rain forest? Many animals like to gobble up crunchy insects and other scrumptious animals. But there are also plenty of vegetarians who munch only leaves, shoots, fruit, and nuts.

Strange but True

A gorilla treats itself to breakfast in bed. It just lies back in its grass nest and picks fresh green leaves from nearby.

A gorilla has a huge appetite. Every day, it spends six hours eating.

"If I don't find my food, I'm going to go nuts!"

Jaw-some!

An agouti is a champion nut-cracker that has incredibly strong jaws. It is one of the few animals that can crack a Brazil nut. The agouti is similar to other rodents because it buries a hoard of nuts to save for later. But the forgetful creature can't always remember where it put them! The lost nuts often sprout up later and grow into trees.

HOME-GROWN LUNCH

"Phew! I need a vacation!"

Leaf-cutter ants work in teams to grow food. One team collects leaves.

"Your turn now!"

Another team chews the leaves until they become a sticky pulp.

Tasty fungus grows on the pulp. The last team harvests the fungus.

"Mmm, fungus. My favorite!"

Cats Go Fishing

Jaguars are the only big cats that live in Central and South America. Unlike many cats, jaguars are happy in water and are strong swimmers. They enjoy eating fish and sometimes even catch crocodiles. They also eat smaller mammals. Jaguars are good climbers and often hide in leafy trees, waiting for their next meal to stroll by. Then they jump down and give their victim a nasty surprise.

That's Weird

Most insects eat plants, but with the pitcher plant it's the other way around. An insect slides from the rim of the plant, into a pool of liquid and drowns. Then the pitcher plant digests it.

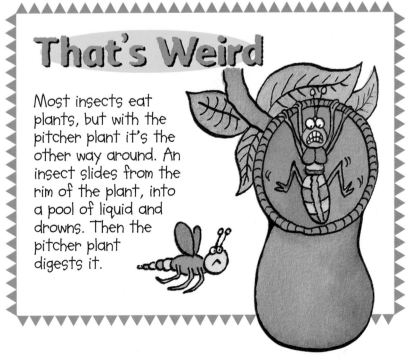

▲ A chameleon glues a victim to its tongue with a sticky glob of spit!

Crafty Chameleon

SNACK ATTACK

In a fraction of a second, the quick-draw chameleon snaps up a tasty insect. The chameleon's tongue is as long as its body!

A chameleon's tongue ▷ can be this super-long!

0 cm 1 2 3 4 5 6
0 inches 1 2

Rainbow Reptile

Imagine being able to change color! In minutes, a chameleon turns from one color to another to blend in with its surroundings and hide from enemies. It also changes color with mood. An angry chameleon has orange patches to let other chameleons know that it's cross!

For My Final Trick!

When all else fails, the chameleon has one last trick to fool enemies. It plays dead. When face to face with danger, it flops to one side, with a limp body, drooping eyelids, and stiff legs. As soon as its enemy turns its back, the chameleon makes a dash for it.

Did that twig just move? Did that leaf just fly away? Rain forest animals are masters of disguise. They have all kinds of tricks to help them catch dinner and to avoid being eaten themselves!

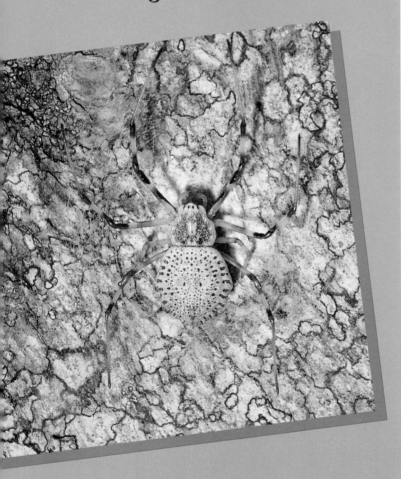

Vanishing Act

The ornate orb-weaver spider flattens itself against the bark of a tree, stays absolutely still and—presto—it seems to disappear. The coloring of the spider exactly matches the moldy, flaky, and mottled colors of the bark.

That's Weird

An orchid mantis is patient and cunning. It looks just like an orchid gently swaying in the breeze. When an insect lands nearby, it pounces.

Bottoms Up!

When this South American frog feels threatened, it shows its attacker an eyeful of the black circles on its backside. The frightened attacker backs off because it thinks that the circles are the eyes of a much larger creature!

Camouflage

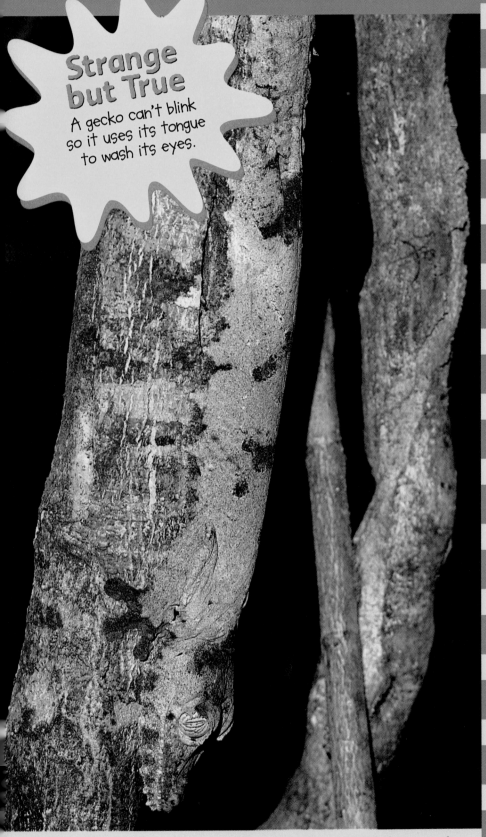

Strange but True

A gecko can't blink so it uses its tongue to wash its eyes.

▲ Look closely to spot the big eyes of a gecko lizard. It has patchy green and brown skin that looks just like bark.

The spiky thornbug looks just like a genuine plant thorn, so most enemies leave it alone.

The walking-stick insect is an experienced actor. It blends in with its surroundings and, if necessary, won't move for up to six hours!

17

Danger!
Red Alert

There's always a watchful predator about, ready to fight to the death. Many animals have ingenious ways of catching prey. They may trap, poison, bite, or even strangle it. Or they may just swallow it up alive.

That's Weird

An ogre-faced spider weaves a web about the size of a postage stamp and waits in ambush. When an insect zooms by, it covers it with the sticky net and delivers a lethal bite.

Viper Swipe!

The eyelash viper fixes its eyes on its target, rotates its fangs at the front of its upper jaw into position, aims, then bites with deadly accuracy. It injects lethal poison straight through its fangs into the prey.

Flying Killers

An eagle is the biggest and fastest flying killing machine in the rain forest. It can spy a monkey in the canopy from over 2 miles (3.2 km) above, swoop down at lightning speed, and snatch it with its razor-sharp talons. Then it flies away to enjoy its meal in peace.

Dinnertime!

Stranglehold

The anaconda is a giant snake that can grow to be as long as six children lying end to end. It wraps its long body around and around its victim, then squeezes tight. The victim can't escape and soon chokes to death.

▲ In double-quick time, the tiny eyelash viper's head darts forward to grab a passing lizard in its big mouth.

Lethal Mini-beasts

Many of the worst killers in the forest are also the smallest. Insects and spiders are top-notch hunters that catch their prey in all kinds of disagreeable ways.

Strong Stink!

The rove beetle has a smart but smelly disguise. It looks like a piece of dung! It hangs around real dung, where it gobbles up flies which are drawn to the smelly stuff. And when there's no dung around, the beetle makes its own stink to lure flies to their doom.

Believe it or Not

Some insects use chemical warfare by spraying enemies with blistering liquid.

Slurping Spiders

A black widow spider is enemy number one to insects. Its venom can be 15 times more deadly than that of a rattlesnake. One small nip from a black widow's needle-sharp fangs and it's all over for an insect. Then, all the spider needs to do is suck out the insect's insides!

WASP VERSUS TARANTULA

The female hawk wasp is a small but daring opponent of the tarantula spider. She dives in bravely.

I must avoid those fearsome fangs!

The wasp injects venom into the spider so that it cannot move, but is still alive. Then...

Ouch! You bully!

...she drags the spider to her nest and lays eggs on it. When the eggs hatch, the babies eat the spider.

Phew! I'm tired but the WINNER!

The praying mantis claps together her two front legs to grip her unfortunate victim.

Munching Mantis

The praying mantis is a calm and calculating killer. She sits extremely still, holding up her front legs as if saying a prayer. But this devious insect is really waiting for a tasty morsel to fly by. The praying mantis is so greedy that she sometimes gobbles up her partner after mating!

What's in a Name?

Battalions of army ants march like real soldiers in search of food. They are fierce hunters that capture and kill.

Batty Bats

Bats are amazing. They are mammals, like you, but they can fly. In the rain forest, you will find bats nesting together in big groups.

▲ Tent bats spend the day snuggled up together resting in preparation for night flights when they search for fruit and insects.

Tree Houses

Tent bats camp out in the understory near trees with fruit. They use large leaves to make cozy, hanging tents. First, the little nibblers bite small holes along either side of the leaf. This bends the leaf to make a roof shape. Then they hook their feet into the holes and hang, heads down, safe from the heat of the sun and out of the wet of the rain.

That's Weird

Fruit bats have their own air-conditioning system. They fan themselves with their big, flappy wings!

It's cozy in here!

23

Life's a Breeze...
Swinging in the Trees

The canopy is full of animal acrobats and trapeze artists. Monkeys, frogs, and snakes leap from tree to tree with incredible ease. They seem to fly through the air—bobbing and tumbling, but never losing their balance.

FLYING SSSSNAKES

Where's that frog going?

It curves itself in an S-shape and soars through the air. The chase is on.

I'm behind you!

It lands safely on a branch. Gulp!

A slippery snake slithers and wriggles, then jumps after its prey.

Branching Out

Monkeys are graceful tree acrobats. They stretch and swing, gripping on to branches with their strong hands and feet. An orangutan can soar huge distances between one branch and the next. But a big, old male orangutan is too heavy to live in the trees, so he retires to the ground and moves on all fours.

Super Glue

Tree frogs have real suction power. Their special fingers and toes stick to slippery tree trunks and branches. They are so sure-footed, they can hang upside-down from a branch without falling off.

Going Up

Scientists who study animals in the rain forest need a head for heights. They use climbing ropes, walkways, and even hot-air balloons to make sure they get a bird's-eye view of what's going on in the treetops.

Squawk!

▲ An orangutan has much longer arms than legs!

25

In the Swim

Huge rivers, such as the mighty Amazon, flow through every rain forest. If you take a peek below the surface of their murky waters, you'll see some creatures that are truly, totally amazing!

It's Shocking!

An electric eel's muscles work like batteries. They make electric signals, which help the eel to find its way around the muddy river and stun its prey. It can zap its victims with up to 650 volts—enough electric power to stun a horse!

I like my fish fried!

Believe it or Not

A crocodile has a pair of see-through eyelids so that it can protect its eyes without closing them.

Open Wide

A crocodile's huge jaws and sharp teeth would scare any dentist. This ferocious reptile lurks with only its eyes and nostrils above the water, waiting for a thirsty animal to come for a drink. SNAP! It opens its huge jaws and the unfortunate creature is dragged underwater to a watery grave.

What's in a Name?

The mudskipper jumps and skips along the muddy shores on strong pectoral fins. It's just as happy living underwater, too.

Gentle Giant

What eats a vast amount of plants each day and looks like a swimming elephant? The manatee. It's the largest rain forest animal and scientists think that it really is a distant relative of the elephant. It swims slowly using its flippers and tears at plants with its long lip.

Under the Microscope

The piranha has rows of needle-sharp teeth. It smells the blood of an injured animal and after finding it, rips it up!

▲ **A manatee knocks sand off a plant, then swallows it whole.**

HA HA! How do electric eels get to work? They take a buzz. HEE HEE!

After Dark

The rain forest is open 24 hours a day. When darkness falls, wide-eyed animals wake up and come out to play!

Hey! It's rude to stare!

A bushbaby's big eyes and excellent hearing help it to find insects and other food at night.

Gaping Gecko

It's easy to lose your way in the dark. Many nocturnal animals, including geckos, have large eyes that let in lots of light. In the daytime, their eyes become narrow slits.

Success Story

A firefly makes light work of finding a mate in the dark. It has a light in its tail that flashes on and off as a mating call!

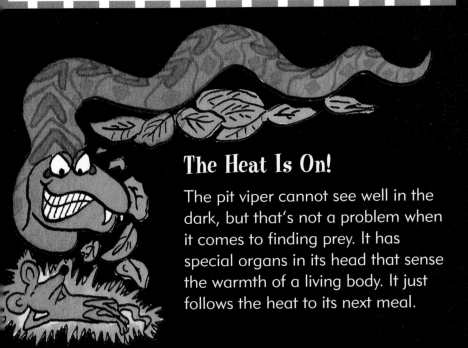

The Heat Is On!

The pit viper cannot see well in the dark, but that's not a problem when it comes to finding prey. It has special organs in its head that sense the warmth of a living body. It just follows the heat to its next meal.

Bats work the night-shift looking for food. The blood-thirsty vampire bat bites birds and mammals with two sharp front teeth. Then it laps up blood from the gaping wounds!

The fishing bat spots a fish's fin sticking up slightly out of the water, then keeps tabs on it with a special tracking system. When the bat is close to the fish, it pounces on its fresh supper.

Prize Day

It's Prize Day in the rain forest and you have a chance to meet even more amazing plants and animals. Some are huge and some are tiny, but every one's a winner!

Fearsome Froggy

The prize for scariest animal goes to arrow poison frogs. They look pretty harmless, but they're the deadliest creatures on Earth. Some have enough poison in their skin to kill 1,000 people.

What a Mouthful

The goliath bird-eating tarantula beats all other spiders for size. Measuring as much as 11 inches (28 cm) from toe to toe, this hairy bird-eater fits nicely across a large dinner plate. Imagine finding this giant spider on the table instead of your lunch!

Beetle That!

The gold medal for weight-lifting goes to the rhinoceros beetle. This colossal creepy-crawly is so strong, it simply lifts up other insects that get in its way, using its pointed horns.

Wonder Wings

You can hardly miss the Queen Alexandra's birdwing in a butterfly parade. The female's wings can measure an incredible 11 inches (28 cm) from tip to tip, making it the largest butterfly in the world.

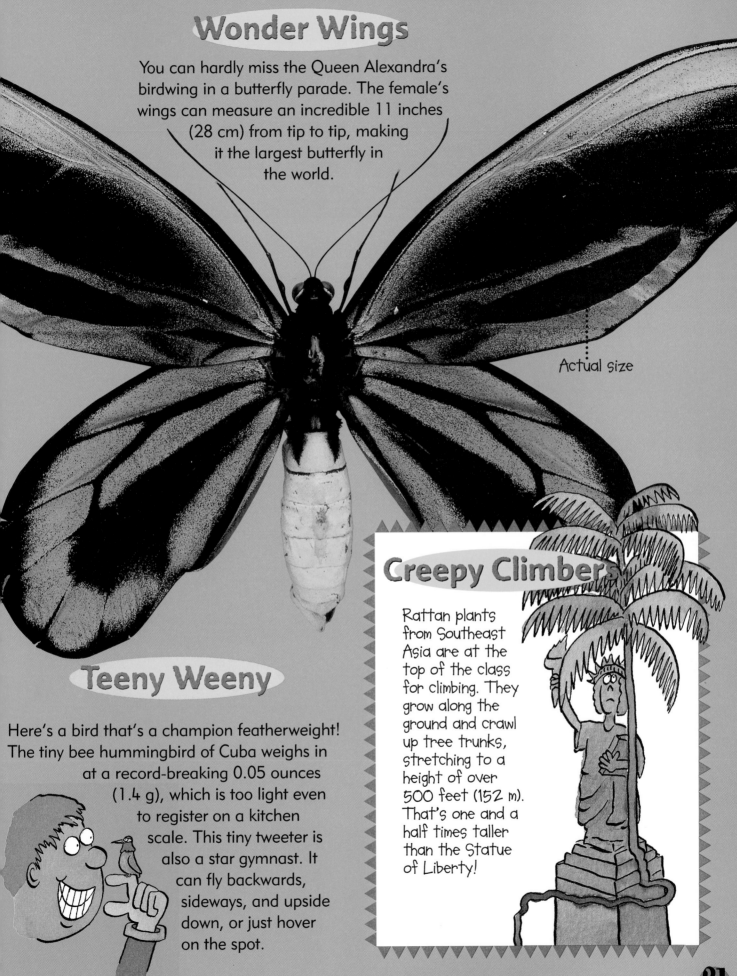

Actual size

Teeny Weeny

Here's a bird that's a champion featherweight! The tiny bee hummingbird of Cuba weighs in at a record-breaking 0.05 ounces (1.4 g), which is too light even to register on a kitchen scale. This tiny tweeter is also a star gymnast. It can fly backwards, sideways, and upside down, or just hover on the spot.

Creepy Climbers

Rattan plants from Southeast Asia are at the top of the class for climbing. They grow along the ground and crawl up tree trunks, stretching to a height of over 500 feet (152 m). That's one and a half times taller than the Statue of Liberty!

Index and Glossary

Illustrations: Woody, Lorna Kent
Consultant: Jonathan Elphick
Author: Kate Graham
Photographs: Cover: Images Colour Library; p1: Robert Harding Picture Library; p3: Robert Harding Picture Library; p4/5: Robert Harding Picture Library; p6: Tony Stone Images; p7: Bruce Coleman Ltd; p8/9: Still Pictures; p9: FLPA; p11: Bruce Coleman Ltd; p12: Planet Earth Pictures; p14/15: Natural History Photographic Agency; p16: Premaphotos Wildlife; p17: Bruce Coleman Ltd; p18/19: Michael & Patricia Fogden; p21: Natural History Photographic Agency; p22/23: Bruce Coleman Ltd; p25: Tony Stone Images; p26: Natural History Photographic Agency; p27: Planet Earth Pictures; p28: Robert Harding Picture Library; p29: Premaphotos Wildlife; p30: Bruce Coleman Ltd; p31: The Natural History Museum, London.